VIATICUM

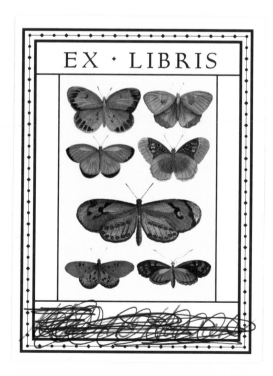

EX · LIBRIS

VIATICUM

HEATHER PYRCZ

GASPEREAU PRESS MMII

provisions taken for use on the journey and now the journey itself

AUDREY THOMAS

to Greg
who always knows the way home

CONTENTS

Prologue

———

Is it lack of imagination that makes us come
to imagined places; not just stay at home
Or could Pascal have been not entirely right
about just sitting quietly in one's room?

TRAVELLING BACKWARDS

To be a traveller
you don't have to journey far—
begin small, say, a street
in your own hometown,
learn the names of people
and how to say hello in their
languages; learn the names
of bushes, a tree, the bird singing
in its unknown branches;
follow the flow of running water
to its source; you will arrive
in the mountains,
breathing the rarefied air,
sleeping deeply,
wondering why it took you
so long to get here

Even the poorest among us journey
like shamen into the past,
or Dante crossing the pass
that never had let any man survive,
into that bitter world for
pure necessity, pure creation.
We scout the future,
a decision to leave or stay (is it
the right one, the right moment
in history?)
We dive into ourselves,
high divers off Mazatlán cliffs
plunging into a chthonic pool
not knowing its depth—its poetic
composition—is it or is it not
a receptacle of light?

GRAFFITI

this art bombs history
burns time
turns art into a verb: SCREW
YOU appears and disappears
like a gesture

someone creeps into the narrow subway tunnel
crawls down its screaming length to plant
icons, tags, scrawled outrage
on the grey walls, obscene
risks claiming I AM
(and I AM NOT)
HERE

I had one once: like Dürer's
            Imagines coelt Meridionate
                        but without resolution
            an angel hovering
(*whom the lone heart*
            has to encounter
                        with so much effort)
            pointing to a place
I almost knew

Postcards from Europe

---

light of the swan-white moon
the blazing light of trees
And the rarely glimpsed bright face
behind the apparency of things

P.K. PAGE

THERE ARE PLACES NO ONE OWNS

(like the heartland of a poem)
the paths of hang-gliders in the Alps
the sculpted pools of the Atlantic
the lonely homes of winter moles

and more—
the leaping chasm of dancers
the nest between a violinist
and her violin, or the used
damp body of legends

THE TAIL END OF THE GROVE

Travelling is always departure;
even after we return,
we don't know where it ends.
At the time, we think we discern the forms:
rose garden, lime tree walk, nut grove,
an old stone tower

(we climb the turret stairs to watch the sunrise)

but what will we know of protean shadows
glimpsed from train windows,
or gleaned on a terrace overlooking
the Côte d'Azur—though brilliant
it's not the azure sea
that we remember

(even from here *the tail end of the grove*
is still in darkness)

A warm spring, the old men are playing boules,
the young lean against the heat on the basketball courts,
Sunday lovers loll in the grass and jealously watch us pass.
Travel gives you an edge, plucks you out of the semi-
transparent envelope of your sleep-walking life
where you are just more atoms in an incessant shower
of atoms, and pastes you like a cardboard cut-out
on the Tour Eiffel.
We go, thinking we'll find places in our memories,
dormant manuscripts, we search graveyards, cloisters, formal
gardens, thinking we'll find luminous names,
old stories, and we do, but they are all of home.

IN MADAM WAREN'S HOUSE

On first glance, Rousseau's room
is modest, a sparse, severe room
with veiled bed, books,
a wooden table—
save for the private door
which opens on turret
      stairs
leading to Madame's chamber.

Did he confess before he played the organ
Sundays in the Savoy Chapel,
or being a young man, heady with the
power of herbs and subversive words,
lean into the priest's ear, whisper
recipes for nightshade and coriander?

ANNA'S ASCENSION

How can we not envy Anna Bach
      (always portrayed as vigourous and good natured,
      always calm and calming Bach,
      singing, in a room austere and unadorned,
      filled with children playing harpsichords,
      cellos, and violins; the younger ones
      sprawled on the floor, watching, waiting
      their turn. Bach, of course, composing
      another cantata, or passion,
      Ascension perhaps,
      or *The Passion of Saint Matthew*,
      oblivious to the distractions, the practice,
      or humming its counterpoint.
      Anna reclines in a rocker,
      picks up her sewing,
      also unconsciously humming)
all that
    music

SOLITAIRE

Sometimes, when Prospect Street is deafening,
a riotous cacophony of jumbled lives,
I envision the Hautes-Alpes and an abbey,
rock face on three sides,
                              a high mountain road
            desolate and risky
                        the scent of chives
                              Inside,
moat resistance, children
disappear down remote corridors
            even their light absorbed
                        into the stone walls

The only sound a delicate bird
            twittering
at nightfall

IN THE MUSÉE D'ORSAY

Pompon's polar bear prowls
the central aisle,
the station clock behind him,
downwind;
he prowls as he does the Bay,
sniffing at the shore's edge
until he knows: today
I walk on water

L'ARENA ROMANA IN ARLES

The outer stonewall crumbles
to the touch, its particles lie like
days in your astonished hand.
In the heart of L'Arena
two thousand years
seep under your skin, confirm
the blazing afternoons,
the fervent flags, blazons, coronets,
the scuffed-up dust of lion and human teeth,
muffled cries resisting death;
then, the relentless emptying of space—
witness the tide that went out and out and out
and never came in.

In Sight of Land

————————

carry a map so worn
it is open to possibility

CAFÉ DE NUIT

Why do we live in common,
gravitate to the twilight
gathering places
bright with seductive light,
music, other bodies?
Because we are theorists, artisans
of space who long to create
out of the raw facts of history
new figures, new constellations,
and between one another
open up the dark, interstellar spaces
a new geography of meaning.

INUKSHUK

You stand in the garden
reconstructed, hand to stone,
from the hungry tundra.
Your singular glance
levels the perennial beds,
the rose garden, berms,
the ornamental trees, pagodas
even the distant fields
——the borrowed vistas——
to desert.
This is how simply
yet completely
you remember

TALKING

I am learning to listen to myself
and watch while I say poverty for property
not missing a beat.

I expose myself like an Ihalmuit shaman
to howling winds and unfathomable
hunger to gainsay.

PROVISIONS

We are seduced into believing meaning
resides in the consumption of things;
render necessary statuary or gilded glass
to fashion ourselves, insist
we need this and this and this
until we can no longer ride the mules up the mountain,
nor cross the pass with our bloated outfit,
falling with it, trapped by an early winter
until wind consumes the remains—
stark reminder for those
who come later

LANDMARKS

In an empty field down Eye Road is
a fence that heaved once, long ago;
nothing remains enclosed
but the quiet poverty.

Fault lines crack by internal pressure
then displace
                    shift stratified layers
a gap is born, wrenched like the throw
and heave of other sites of power.

Oh, to avoid the precipitous cliff,
quagmire, thicket,
laying siege to the walled city,
the benefit of the brilliant strategist;
and yet, we still do it—we turn fifty.
Plato promised
this is when you'll have
your vision of The Good.

I waited patiently all morning—
not knowing what to expect,
hoping it wouldn't be too
abstract. Then, just past noon,
when the clear September sky
was at its bluest,
Tess and I spotted five bald eagles
soaring over Grand Pré,
in sight of the Bay, the tide rising,
the fields of corn and sunflowers
burnished gold below.

PARALLEL LIVES

Sometimes I miss the sixties,
the wanton days and boundless nights—
sneaking out, smoking up,

driving the mountain road,
wailing every song on Highway 61
your hand inside my thigh.

I know they say it wasn't like that,
not in the sociology or glum faces
of the children of the seventies,

but in this time of debt,
          restraint,
sacrifice

of curb and drag, denial and arrest,
of resignation then regret, when all
is withholding, *no, nay*

I miss the days of dancing
          in the street
                    in a long thin dress

CALAMITY'S CHILDREN

to Al Purdy

I wanted to tell you
> when I wandered out of the north,
> 17, lost, a stranger in my own country,
> clutching a couple of arctic rhododendrons,
> telling myself that if university
> felt like Marilyn's residential school,
> (*you are not good enough, not good enough,*
> *obviously not good enough*)
> perhaps I, too, could be self taught
that I needed you
(as the hero needs Tiresius)
to say "here is the road."

I am one of the guilty trying to acknowledge
my guilt, not knowing how
to start, not knowing where
my own stops and history begins.

I'm hoping to talk to you,
having come through
Persephone's entrance,
at the blood pit, the best place
for heroes and lovers and
others who need to know
what not to kill by accident
or folly or hatred or
indifference.

I need the way home, now
that we are all calamity's children
having failed Jerusalem.

FOR RILKE

Andante

She walks the dyke. October.
The water is purple with bruised
shadows, the black ducks
line the icy edge oblivious
to the warning call of geese,
the sea grass turns the dusky hue
of winter wheat.
The crops are all in, the last
rejected corn lies down, rots.
A solitary heron flies close and low,
his great grey wings
skimming the water.

Allegro grazioso

She walks the dyke, stunned
at how easily burning towers collapse
and wonders whose sword blade
will flicker in what light—
are any of us innocent?
She walks the dyke as if in dream,
dredging the conundrums,
strip mining the heart.
She walks out beyond the murmurings of town,
past the reservoir turns toward Grand Pré,
starts down the railroad tracks,
stops. Walking is too fast,
is not enough.

Coda: lente e placido

She stands still,
turns her face to the wind
that crosses and recrosses the land.
If she walks far enough, stands still
long enough, she sees herself.
She doesn't like what she sees,
waits for absolution,
an invisible peace that says
stand as still as this hawthorn
and cling

this is the necessity
    of solitude

Flying Dreams

I should have begun with this: the sky
A window minus sill, frame, and panes.
An aperture, nothing more,
but wide open.

WISLAWA SZYMBORSKA

ELEMENTARY PARTICLES

The skateboarders
fly up the wall
like waves against a cliff
rolling, folding back as unharmed;
do we expect them to shatter like light on water?
They defy gravity, coherence,
breathing in air lit with fire
their eyes pure defiance.

In practice,
jumping off the stone steps
of the elementary school,
twisting a stalwart pirouette,
their cries, grunts, squeals
crack open a possibility—
a different universe.

FIFTH GEAR

Where are we going today, I ask,
waiting for the engine to fire,
her hand on the wheel to steady,
waiting for her right hand to shift
into reverse, back up from where
we are now safely sitting,
roar into first—second—louder
where are we going today—third—
I have something to show you
something you haven't seen yet—
fourth—fifth—sweet jesus, I pray,
may her hand steady.
The mountain is a wall before us,
I count the telescoping trees,
we leave the ground gaining speed,
Oh no—the universe again—
what am I supposed to see?

SPIRIT BEAR

rare as the snow leopard,
luminous among the rocks and fallen
pine along the black rivers,
weaving among the cello mountains,
the flute streams,
dreaming of flying fish,
sweet roots, succulent berries
        —untouchable nakedness
        unconscious bliss—
when we catch a glimpse of you
like falling stars or unicorns
(once there were unicorns)
we weep, astonished at our own
inner immaculate wilderness

Raven commiserates with us
in dreams. He too knows
the limits of language.

He perceives the sky indigo blue,
the earth stained ochre red,
himself as divine.

What are we to Raven but mere mortals
who walk the earth and weep
at the abyss.

Last night, Raven flew into my dreams,
his great black beating wings
spoke intimately of love's knowledge,

how sky needs earth and god needs mortal
recognition, and every beating heart
needs the other to say: this is the true self.

Yet this morning I am alone and speechless,
hear only his raucous *caw caw*
from the flaming maple.

FIVE FINGER RAPIDS

I passed the dangerous place,
the suspension bridge slung
over the rapids between
two peaceable territories,
two peaceable kingdoms:
innocence and resignation.

You stand on the bridge—
clinging to the frayed, knotted rope,
forgetting other tenures, other dispensations,
hearing only the roar of the chaotic
waterfall rushing down a dark chasm
dragging you in—nothing between
but rope and mist.

What can be heard over the roar
but the recognition of our child's voice
on the crowded playground, the sound
of a lover's moan, the touch of a hand
that cuts through nightmare sleep
and grounds us.

CHAIN SMOKING

This holy flame held between
pierced lips, the trance-maker,
delays the awakening, the reckoning
of daily life, prevents falling, leaping.
Suspended above the well of despair,
she lights one from the other
like white candles on the altar,
afraid to break the spell.

ACT OF CREATION

Look at her rapturous face
above the blossoming roundness

Ah! how I long to be, once more, among
that angelic order of complete inwardness

as if I alone were being rained on
in the midst of unbearable heat

You read my words, but do not love me.
No, don't explain, I understand you
read my words, but don't embrace me.
Unlike another who rejected
all the choices, roles, showed only
contempt for plodding minds,
who would not bend to kiss even children,
but stands hangdog and does not know
why they will not love her, I understand
what's written on your face—
I'm not a nurse, no doctor, won't service you
in any way, no Florence, no Madame Curie
nor will I sacrifice myself for any of my
great loves, no Joan, no Juliette, no Virginia
I will not hide my contempt in carnival jest,
no Jane, nor confess my pain, no Anne, no Sylvia
nor will I hide myself away, no Emily
I see it in your eyes, my words are cold edged,
can't live in your house, mustn't survive
to execute or supplant or even revise.
Well, undoubtedly, you will try to
fill my mouth with stones and knives,
drive a stake and force me to the ground,
but I will fly

Psychic Rifts

Meanwhile, civilization was removing man further and further from his instinctual foundation, so that a gulf opened between nature and mind, between the unconscious and consciousness. These opposites characterize the psychic situation that is seeking expression in modern art.   CARL JUNG

I fear the trembling air, the restless motion
the pacing back and forth, back and forth.
Shush! Let it begin: Santarem, Santos,
Catacomb, Hill of Skeleton, House of Bedlam—
        here she comes
When did I get so far from water?

Oh, I don't know if it's right—this calling up—
this autopsy. What if we expose mystery to the eroding air?
Come away! And leave ambiguity an escape instead
of an opened and shut door. I think Elizabeth weeps
at our clumsy handling. 'We dwindle into prose.'

Nonsense, your time is short, ask your questions:
I fear the nature of our language, our sightings,
Elizabeth, do we speak, remember the perfect past?
A text told in end-stop prose, a conclusion buried
in the archives? No, it is a story forever being told:
I was leaving, I am leaving, I will be leaving
doors closing and reopening, a porthole turning inside
out. The clasped hand/eye lives, dreams, writes
the continuous past

Where were you going, that time in Brazil,
thinking of travelling, travelling

and the trees gesturing
Where am I going but home?
The roads deep in snow
the higher we go, the flatter the landscape
becomes, until we have a map seen. Islands
become continents, continents become islands.
I've set the surface in motion, a wave theory,
carrying me where I need to go. The compass
is a small boat on the hell-green sea.

I hear the day-springs of the morning strike.
Where is she going? Wait now, she's leaving.
another departure. You cannot follow.
These are the years and the walls and the doors

son rythme est mort comprend

We enter the ramp— like a poem
the ancient stone prepares us
for visions   voices
Light from a cathedral
window
          wavers
les trois sorcières
draw their magic circle.

In the grey granite dusk
material bodies fade,
the mind reaches for vaulted chambers
(close the circle, think
like stone and blue velvet).

We dance up the ramp
breathing the rarefied air.
          There is a wind on Lake Nemi
the gulls are screeching
          despite the setting sun.
Fuseli's Belinda breathes heavily
and   everywhere   the sound
of Venus plucking Cupid's wings.

Musing in the Great Hall
   the mind slips through smoke
     glass doors,
       passages.
          Inside
questions:
who fled the virgin forest
       what floats in the River Wye, at dusk
why Qualupiluk is weeping
       hours fall
          away
lost in the echoes
       Terre sauvage
mirrored chambers, pools, the marble halls.

We exit down the ramp
   as calm as water lapping
     at the walls of Ljsselstein.

Outside,
a green ceiling,
a sheltering sky.

OTTAWA, 1992
FOR LOU P. COLE

54

MATISSE'S ICARUS

is neither flying nor falling.
It is the moment (suggested
by the articulation of his head)
he realizes, amid the stars,
he is equal to the sun.
That's why, I think,
his heart beats so red.
I suppose it explodes,
his swan dive pouring out
tumultuous dreams;
nor does it matter
what others read into
his white legs disappearing,
as by the time he hits the water
he is already dead.

LA FORÊT DE SYMBOLES

Listen my dears—how softly night arrives

We enter the intimate *forêt* like
a hobbit in the enchanted wood,
searching for the ineffable—
a path and the need to stay on it.
But to the right and to the left
are glimmering, insubstantial lights,
shimmering and elusive,
and strands of music, laughter,
the leaping flicker of firelight.

We try to follow the reedy woodsman,
his clear high register, trusting
his knowledge of signs, his acute
observations, green harmonies;
but we are drawn to the diffused light,
the amber, musk, the aromatic resin—
why do we desire the forbidden?

What do we expect amid stone ruins
hidden in the oak trees
but the grotesque, the misbegotten,
sullen, belied by laughter,
their distorted edges blurred
by clamorous music
and shadows thrown from the darkness.

We are attracted and repulsed
at our own dark imaginings,
doubting our capacity for pain,
for mutinous surrender—
what could we say of comfort?
But something draws us on,
inceptive, vernal possibilities.

Perhaps it is a band of gypsies,
off the road for the night, foraging,
bathing in the reservoir
of the *anima mundi*—do you hear water?
staving off the dark with their cocked guns
and prophetic tambourines,
their oncoming sight,
music echoing off the water.

Our companion calls us back. We stumble,
tripped by a thought:
this, too, is an abyss with a cold wind,
creates vertigo by its very window
on the infinite.

Again the woodsman—we plead
with him over our shoulder,
    what if it's our aboriginal selves
singing, drumming and this is
a homecoming—

what then? Not to stray!
How will we ever find
(amid the showers
of bright tears)
our prophet-tribe?

BALLADE, OP. 10, NO. 2

1.

At a low table in his room
in the Carlgasse,
a frugal Brahms begins
his day at 5 A.M. with a cup
of his own strong coffee

> (muses, mulls the dark dance
> a gypsy night of revelling that
> mutates to folklore told of enigmatic
> wounds, murder, accidents—
> hawkable on a London street)

He puts down his cup,
rejects the overwrought ballad,
its dance halls and other lurid
associations, dreams
of *a naked soul*
pure and unashamed

Perhaps the slow increment
of events— birth, marriage, death
and death and death
takes him to this place
where the solo voice mutes
becoming
absolute
music

2.

Night fast falling—the bittersweet birds
vanish, stilled by the outer dark. Even the massed
voices coming from the Innere Stadt are lost.
The only sound is the braying of the wind,
elliptic strands, B minor, truncated—
I know this song. Robert played it one
winter's night. Clara and I in the kitchen
(I was slicing onions with a sharp knife)
"Go on with what you're doing," Robert said,
"I'll play you something new." New, yes
but brooding vast and so oppressive
I dropped the knife, slicing open my hand.
Who recalls these unsubstantial sensations?
Clara gasped, wrapped it; I, tranced, oblivious
to her touch, walking with Eusebius—
Robert's alter ego, his haunted self
     ask: *woher, warum, wohim*

Only emotion endures.
Clara and I go on year after year
catching songs, imperfect cadences, in the wind,
like the soft whistling in his corner of the
Kaffeebaum

Earth Air Fire Water

———————————

SACRED PLACES

1.

In the beginning, before Earth, at its conception
when everyone was behind the veil of ignorance

and no one had to wonder what the archangel
thought, we could only imagine (in the Eye of God)

how exquisite and articulate, how pristine,
how full of moral choice Earth would be

2.

I do not know much about gods, but I am afraid
in the moment of invocation, before I explain

my intentions (*beg for mercy*). In that instant
is a chasm of time when everything is remembered,

the history of all bodies, and I have not yet
suspended the bridge that might allow passage

3.

What do we see in a single rotation,
we are so accustomed to creation, to magic

no longer amazed at the rising sun,
we ignore its divinity, being too sublime,

we draw our yantras on rock walls
dream a secular perfection

4.

When Rome was conceived, Romulus sent for
the Etruscans, to instruct him in the mysteries

First they dug the Mundus, a pit
and threw in ripe fruit as an offering,

each man tossing a handful of earth from his
own land to mingle in the foundation

Drawing a circle for the city's boundary
with a plow drawn by a bull and a cow

Romulus squared the circle with two impossible
arteries that ran out to the four gates of the city

We're told they met at the abode of the ancestors,
covered by a great stone, the soul stone

which sings with voices, a three-part invention
of the living and the dead and the dying

5.

On certain days, even now, when the stone is removed
the dead rise from the shaft to walk among the living

Who remembers this sacred place
where we are bound to the other world?

I am aware of the days, only by voices,
chthonic shadows gently mocking my indifference

A NECESSARY DARKNESS

*You do not have to sit outside in the dark. If, however, you
want to look at the stars, you will find darkness is necessary.*
ANNIE DILLARD

1.

How deep the universe, how dark and filled with light

What comes after myth, after the tale about the woman
and the beast, the jaded field, the lonely hill, the tree

that opens up but only once;
all of it is there in the stars, our unholy past

we like the past writ large; but what comes
after Beatrice shows Dante the multifoliate rose

what's left to fill the void, besides the nebulae
and other ethereal showers streaming across the sky

just stars and stars and stars

2.

I'm standing on the last corner of land,
it runs down to the sea, a pebble beach

It's night, pre-dawn, and I am alone
I've walked down here in my sleep

I'm trying to find a path to the stars; tonight
the Milky Way is brilliant, so

close. I want to enter the breathing, wandering
Stygian dark: there's something there I need

The wet grass, stones don't wake me. I suppose
I expect the planets to be stone cold

Only the lapping of the Atlantic at my knees
and a voice that found me absent

between two parting dreams
awakens me

3.

you can be weaned / from the things of the world
RILKE

Some nights when we think—I could tonight
I could sleep out under the stars

wrapped perhaps in Cygnus wings, swept up,
enveloped, enfolded in bright arms, drawn

an empyrean shawl—we sense behind the stars
there's something infinite imprisoned

in our limits (the cruelty of families, the misery
of cities, the incomprehensibility of law)

lying under the inscrutable sky we touch the sweet
possibility of the infinite something, and the weight

of misery holding us down, but if for one instant we
let go into the tremendousness, into the weightless

universe (one song), wouldn't we lose ourselves?
(we're so afraid, so suckled to the weight, we turn away)

4.

You may perceive Uksawnee as simply luminous
atmospheric phenomenon, aurora borealis,

a luminous arc lying across the magnetic meridian
or filaments, streamers, fans, flames, auroral clouds

triggered by a solar wind, atomic particles
emanating from sunspots, but then

you've never heard them sing, never whistled and banged
and begged them to bend down, never believed

you could make them, this longest of nights, dance to your
tune, reach down almost touch you, before you run inside

you see, Inuit children believe that if the hovering
flaming Uksawnee touch you, you die

We never perceive anything fully, nor comprehend
completely, the rest depends on dreams

5.

Just standing on earth under a night sky is a journey
of vast undertaking. On the sea, tundra, plains

the first thing we did was name the stars
Orion going down, or Venus rising

Something happens at night—the buffer blue sky
disappears and a universe comes crashing in

We don't mind, we like the stars close, we long
to bind, bate, engrave them, make them our own

We're still hunters tracking, explorers extravagantly
lost in the uncharted archipelagos, the trackless waste

What do we know of rift valleys, of the celestial
floor spreading away from its centre

or the violent phases of the moon's craters
or the long dark tracts between the stars

Just standing on earth under a night sky is a journey
so dangerous we might never get back

1. Sacrificial Fire

How easily we call down our own death,
how easily the gods play us in this,

take Agamemnon and his sacrificial vow to Artemis
so carelessly made—what is one beautiful thing?

Until it is yours, a daughter, part goddess
who must be sacrificed as most beautiful

How nobly he refused, but at Aulis with others
blaming him, what then? For a favourable wind

he relents, places her on the sacrificial pyre
—what else could Clytemnestra do? She too

calls down fire

2. *Forest Fire*

There's an acrid smell in the air tonight
like it's coming from South Mountain,

but the news says it's a diuturnity away,
a wall of fire in the New Brunswick wood:

a long funeral pyre, and this wake on the wind
stays all night and into the next day

Even though the fire's burning elsewhere
all you crave is rain in the trees,

the leaves shuddering, a drumming on roofs,
and in the streets long, cool, running rivulets

but rain seems even farther than fire
(you convince yourself you can't breathe)

Three days, the wind has driven
the stench into every nook and cranny,

like dust on the prairies in the thirties
Somewhere this choking air is thicker still,

black smoke billowing—and someone is
full of fear, appalled not only of pine

but towns burning, houses, crops, livestock,
violate clothes on a line, telephone wires,

birds burning, books burning, photographs,
even the fire trucks. Thinking with Buddha—

all, all is burning

3. *Fire Sermon*

My mother fears fire irrationally,
having lived in a mining town

where houses often leapt up and fell back
burning, there was so much drinking,

so much anger glowing below the surface,
emerging to sit on Gran's front stoop

The town's black ash streets smoldered
with poverty and oblivion

Aunt Deedee's expectations
reborn each false-prophesizing dawn

As a child I confused the smell of coal
and the smell of fire—one lit, one stored

in the basement, permeating the clapboard house
with the reek of compressed life about to speak

in flames. A long way away, in the city,
my mother collapses the two—coal or fire—

will ignite grief and pain, despair and
lamentations—somewhere she has to escape;

I, on the other hand, want to be cremated—
how else can we fly up as birds of paradise?

4. *Firewall*

I want to apologize for not containing it—
(Mom's, Gran's, Great Gramma's)

You were only three when Front Street
burned, café, pet store, toy store

every shop up to the firewall—
one day standing, the next levelled

We were all drawn like Promethean moths
to the charred, smoking remains,

the gaping hole. You burst into tears
and cried for three days without stopping,

a day for each year you trusted
in the permanence of things

5. St Elmo's Fire

*fight to recover what has been lost and found
and lost again and again*   ELIOT

We sit, waiting for fire,
like Mom and Gran and

all the women before them,
for our nemesis and our release

It's started, somewhere the flint
is struck, up leaps

the wicked, redeeming flame,
it dreams, racing across ditches,

profane and sacred fields,
soars in skeleton trees,

crossing continents in less than
an age. In our rocking chairs

on the old verandah, the vision
comes *The Holy War is on its way,*

the plague. They will bury us
dig up our bones and burn

them again or have them hanged
Martyrs, catalysts, we wait for fire

This is the way of visions
the unvoiced voice that sounds like the past,

but falls like fireballs from the future—
messages left on walls in ash

DEEP SEAS

My God! I hope that I never have to go
Voyaging anywhere over the sea in winter

1.

Out beyond the Inside Passage, in open water
where one can not discern the sea

from the piercing, impenetrable dark,
a lanterned fleet of fishing boats

dories and trawlers no bigger than the shell of Venus
plunges, lolls, rolls out of sight

then up the fleet rises, a soprano's
wild arpeggio and breathless trill

In this deep dark sea, the improvising heart
must blindly learn its tempo and its pitch

wedded to vast mystery

2.

It frightens me, the sea
God, you are vast

a winter Nor'easter, breaking seas,
a wave rears up, higher than the rest

a rogue—a wall two hundred and nineteen feet,
a wave no one has ever seen and lived,

toppled by the moving air; a roaring Niagara
just wind and sea and a rogue wave breaking

a towering leviathan between you, me, our boat
and where we are and are not

Even on a calm day, the Bay with its bright flotilla
can summon terror

3.

Imagine being set adrift in the Atlantic,
at what point would you sense the immensity,

three thousand miles of water, knowing what inhabits
the sea—shelves, basins, rift valleys

What would you hear besides the lapping
against your body—you, a foreign object

in the everyday flow of complex patterns,
the ocean's ahuman concerto

Could one express a world, manage rogue waves,
hunt food, cultivate water gardens happily,

learn to love unstable ground, extol fluidity,
transparency, an ability to float through history

All adaptations are plausible,
except the freezing solitude

4.

What made Hart Crane leap from his homecoming
Ship or Kees from the Golden Gate Bridge—

was it clarity born of travel and isolation,
a solitary journey over water

or is it something lonelier still
like Frank O'Hara's accident on Fire Island

Are they careless, the poets, of places not contained
by firewalls, jumping into the dark as if it were

a fiction, insisting on the impossibility
of separateness

5.

We journey inward and outward, like the ebb and flow
of tides, we ride the flux of thought, image, memory

of the waking mind—the wave of consciousness,
Virginia's fish: a traveller who never arrives

Yet how close we stay to familiar shores
(lest in the midst of deep sea, one finds oneself

unprepared to continue and unable to return)
bound by the inconstant contours of the land

ACKNOWLEDGEMENTS

I would like to thank Andrew Steeves, Greg Pyrcz and Clare Goulet for
their attentiveness and skill in editing, and for their generosity of spirit;
and Andrew for the creative design of the book; and Tessa Pyrcz for
her careful editing of my use of foreign languages; and all the staff at
Gaspereau Press for their unfailing support and good humour.

Some of the poems were previously published in *Gaspereau Review*,
Canadian Woman Studies, *Vernissage* and The National Gallery's audio
guide. CBC commissioned "La Forêt de Symboles" and "Ballade, Op. 10,
No. 2" for *Take Five*'s "Inspired Words."

AFTERWORD

The map on the book's cover is "Imagines coelt Meridionates," the first printed map of the stars of the southern hemisphere, produced by Albrecht Dürer, a German painter.

The epigraph for the PROLOGUE is from Elizabeth Bishop's "Questions of Travel."

IO SOL UNO is from Dante's *Inferno*, "And I myself/alone prepared to undergo the battle/both of the journeying and the pity" (Cantos II, 3–6).

GRAFFITI refers to Ellen Handler Spitz's "An Insubstantial Pageant Faded: A Psychoanalytic Epitaph for the New York Subway Car Graffiti," in *Post Modern Perspectives*, edited by Howard Rizatti.

I WISH I HAD A MAP FOR THIS JOURNEY refers to Dürer's map, drawn from studies made in Southern Europe and from exciting new observations made by sailors during the first voyages of discovery south of the equator.

The italics in I WISH I HAD A MAP FOR THIS JOURNEY are a quotation of Rilke's *Duino Elegies, No. 1*.

THE TAIL END OF THE GROVE refers to a haiku by Issa.

WALKING DOWN THE CHAMPS DE MARS refers to Virginia Woolf's "Moments of Being."

The epigraph opening the section IN SIGHT OF LAND is from Janet MacAdams' "advice to travellers II."

CAFÉ DE NUIT is a response to Michael Certeau's *Culture in the Plural*.

PROVISIONS refers to Baudrillard's concept of the culture of consumption found in Maggie O'Neil's *Culture and Feminism*.

The first stanza of SEPT. 7, 2001 refers to Gary Geddes' poem "The Terracotta Army."

CALAMITY'S CHILDREN refers to Marilyn Dumont's *Memories of a Really Good Brown Girl*, Al Purdy's poem "Remembering Hiroshima" and Isaiah 65:17–25.

I first came across the myth used in FLYING WOMAN in Betsy Warland's collection, *What Holds Us Here*.

RAVEN AND THE FOURFOLD WORLD refers to Heideggar's fourfold world: earth, air, divinities and mortals.

PSYCHIC RIFTS: "From the psychological standpoint, the two gestures toward the naked object (matter) and the naked object (spirit) point to a psychic rift that created its symbolic expression in the years before the catastrophe of the First World War. This rift had first appeared in the Renaissance, when it became manifest as a conflict between knowledge and faith. Meanwhile, civilization was removing man further and further from his instinctual foundation, so that a gulf opened between nature and mind, between the unconscious and consciousness. These opposites characterize the psychic situation that is seeking expression in modern art" (Carl Jung).

LA FORÊT DE SYMBOLES is a response to James Campbell's recording of Debussy's "Première Rapsodie."

BALLADE OP. 10 NO. 2 is a response to Glen Gould's recording of Brahms "Ballade Op. 10, No. 2." *Woher, warum, wohim* translate whence, wherefore, whither and are the three questions Brahms told his students to ask of the Maker for inspiration.

SÉANCE is a response to a conference on Elizabeth Bishop held at Acadia University in 1998.

THE NATIONAL GALLERY was written in 1992 and refers to a contemporary installation by Anish Kapoor in the gallery at the time. It is dedicated to another artist, Lou P. Cole.

Section 1 of SACRED PLACES refers to John Rawls "veil of ignorance" in *Theory of Justice*; Section 2 refers to T. S. Eliot and Annie Dillard; Section 3 refers to Carl Yung's definition of yantra (a form of mandala, which is the symbol of wholeness, but one that is purely geometrical in design); According to Plutarch, Romulus sent for the builders from Etruria to instruct him in the sacred ceremonies for creating Rome, which is referred to in Section 4.

A NECESSARY DARKNESS is dedicated to E. Alex Pierce and her star-studded home where I had my sleepwalking vision. Section 4 refers to *Inuit Journey* by Edith Iglauer.

Section 1 of FIREWALLS refers to Alistair MacLeod's "As Birds Bring Forth the Sun."

Section 2 of DEEP SEAS refers to Silver Donald Cameron's *The Living Beach*; Section 3 refers to Kafka's "Freezing Solitude"—the loneliness of the writer; Section 5 refers to Dante, *Paradiso* Canto No. 11, 31–33.

A NOTE ON THE TYPE

This book is typeset in Adobe Octavian. Octavian was designed by Will
Carter (1912–2001) and David Kindersley (1915–95) and was originally
released for metal composition by the Monotype Corporation in 1961.
Kindersley was an inscriptional stone cutter who apprenticed under Eric
Gill before setting up his own studio near Cambridge, England. While
teaching a letter-cutting course at the Cambridge Technical College,
Kindersley instructed Will Carter, a fellow stonecutter and the founder of
Rampant Lions Press. When Kindersley suggested that Rampant Lions
Press should have a typeface of its own, Carter invited Kindersley to
collaborate on a design. The result was Octavian, a type whose strong
roman capitals reflect a love for lettershapes inscripted in stone, yet whose
tight-fitting lowercase makes it an economical typeface for book work. The
companion italic was designed by Will Carter. Octavian was adapted for
photo typesetting in 1976, and was first released in digital form in 1990.
This version was supplied by Adobe Systems, Mountain View, California.

Typeset in Adobe Octavian by Andrew Steeves and printed offset at Gaspereau Press by Gary Dunfield and Marilyn MacIntyre.

Gaspereau Press acknowledges the support of the Canada Council for the Arts.

1   3   5   7   6   4   2

NATIONAL LIBRARY OF CANADA CATALOGUING IN PUBLICATION DATA

Pyrcz, Heather Elizabeth, 1951–
Viaticum : poems

ISBN 1-894031-57-1

1. Title.

PS8581.Y73V43 2002   C811'.54   C2002-901333-X
PR9199.3.P97V43 2002

GASPEREAU PRESS, PRINTERS & PUBLISHERS
ONE CHURCH AVENUE, KENTVILLE, NOVA SCOTIA
CANADA B4N 1K7